Four Quarters to a Section

An anthology of South Dakota poets selected in the South Dakota State Poetry Society 2013 manuscript competition. Judged by Gary Dop.

Acknowledgements

Edited by Lawrence Diggs and Rosemary Dunn Moeller

Cover, interior art, book design and layout by Lawrence Diggs

This publication has been generously supported by a grant from the South Dakota Humanities Council.

Rosemary and I have had a lot of help with this project from many people, most notably the South Dakota State Poetry Society's board members. Many thanks to all of you.

Library of Congress Control Number: 2013922018
ISBN   978-0-9912794-0-1

Some of the poems in this collection have been previously published.

By Barbara Duffey
"Aubade with a Quincy Jones Biography on PBS": Barrelhouse, 2007
"Summer Night, Houston": Faultline, Spring 2007
"We Can Definitively Report that We Have Not Released Man-Eating Badgers in the Vicinity": BlazeVOX, Fall 2010
"Scabies": Indiana Review, Winter 2004
"I Run Errands by Myself," "How to Bake the Famed Cushion Cake, Requisite for Bridal Showers and a Favorite of Our Staff," "Lauds": Passages North, Winter/Spring 2011
"Combo, Per the Norm": Prairie Schooner, Spring 2008
"How Simple Machines Work": New Orleans Review, Fall 2011
"Wheel & Axle," "Cento: 'Instinct,' by Lester Del Rey": Sugar House Review, Fall 2012
"Diesel Engine": Western Humanities Review, Summer 2012

By Rosemary Dunn Moeller
"Pintail Ducks Doing It in the Spring": 605 Magazine:
"Too Many Apples": Broadkill Review
"Drought Defiance in Blue": Encore, NFSPS
"Envious While Leaving Innis Mor on the Ferry": Feile Festa
"Above Pearl Creek", "Black Flight Against Blue Sky", "Mates for Life", "Perseids and Pheasants After Dark", "Rock Picking", "Puffins at the Cliffs of Mohr": Pasque Petals, SDSPS
"Sketching Decaying Leaves": Prairie Winds

Editors' Notes

Please note that this is a poetry book. While a strict English teacher might find some punctuation, grammar or spelling in these poems objectionable, it is important to note that various poets use various dictionaries and style guides. There is also a long tradition of "poetic license." I did not require the poets to "rewrite" their poems to make the English teachers happy. That said, I hope that English teachers can also enjoy these great poems.

Some people may quibble that the Bull Terrier is not a Bulldog. According to The Bulldog Information Library and Bulldogbreeders.com, the Bull Terrier is considered a Bulldog.

Table of Contents

Dave Diamond
Musings on the Meanings of Life

Hometown

You walk this old main street, the peeling
board fronts, ferruginous brick, the empty,
fire-torched spaces between the buildings;

no one store the way it was back then, back
when you grew up with Charlie Higgins, Clutch
Klotz, Sonny Sorensen, Arlen Olson; back when

Charlie gave you scarlet fever--dark, hot
weeks of sweating quarantine in the hospital.
You think about this town, the characters--

Hook Ryder, Elmer Witt, town drunks; those
senile, rummy players at the Palace Pool Hall;
old Lady Larson, the crazy cake maker; Wanda

Beasley, who owned the Cozy Cafe, sold beer
to minors, danced with a shot glass on her
head, and ran the cat house out back. You

remember how the town tolerated these misfits
but never forgave Charlie Higgins, the product of
a cousin marriage, reclusive mother, drunken

father, who worked in the lumber yard down by
Ernie's Esso station. They were out to get
Charlie from the beginning, isolated him, like

our quarantine, on the fringe of the community
fabric. Even your own parents warned you
about Charlie and what happens when cousins
marry. You remember how kids baited Charlie

made fun of him, teased, called him a *crazy*,
challenged him to fights; remember back in

high school when Charlie finally split apart,
swiped the school bus, raced down main street,
and crashed into the double doors of the county

court house. He got three years in the reform
school. You stroll this street now, and your
mind turns to the night the carnival set up

here, the grinding merry-go-round, the cranking
Ferris wheel, the tent games, the mustard-smell
of the midway; how you and Charlie Higgins,

both just 13, crawled like commandos to the
back of the girlie show, lifted the tent flap,
and peeped in. Crawled right down that side

street where the Red Owl used to be. Charlie
was the only one who took the dare. He stood
lonely, an outcast on the edge of the group,

winking at you, looking like James Dean. You
walk farther down the street past the Palace
Pool Hall, the front boarded, a rusty Squirt

sign hanging from the door. You squint into
the dirty window, hear the kiss of billiard
balls and remember how that reform school got

to Charlie; how he busted out one night, and
how the talk the next morning at the Cozy Cafe
had it he was on his way back to kill a local.

A week later, a farmer found him dead from eating
green corn in the middle of a field where he'd
been hiding down by the Nebraska state line.

Made in the Midwest

She waddled when she walked
and had a butt like the top
of a silo. She was a few
pounds shy of being a circus
act. There were two women
with her who had pasty faces
and triple chins. They sat
in the booth like barrels,
ordered meatloaf special
with a plate of buttered buns.
The waiter took their order,
then they chatted about where
they might shop later. The
one with the silo-ass yawned,
and through her grotesque,
twisted face-mask, said: *The
radio says K-Mart is the place,
so we'll go there first.*

Summer Fugue

It only takes half an hour
To walk the curve on my side
Of the lake, from the winding

Turn at the historic, log cabin,
Through the tunnel of green trees
Along Lakeshore Road, the ratty

RV park, the colorful women in
Pant suits, tired men in seed
Hats, past the old, public dock

Where a young girl in a black
Bikini takes sun; past the picnic
Tables, the famous Cobblestone

Ballroom, featuring Orville Von
Segren and his band this Saturday
At the Leon and LaDonna Clutter

Wedding dance. From the ballroom
One walks the shoulder of the road
Beside the cabins, the soggy earth
Full of fat, wiggling nightcrawlers,
Down along the bend at the spillway,
Around the roaring waterfall that

Splashes white, foamy spray on the
Slick rocks below, You can get down
There, under the low-hanging branches,

Down where the water spills onto the
Rocks, where lost fish flop over the
Mossy wall, and look straight up into

The sky, see the silver-soot clouds
Open and close like a catcher's mitt.
If you go farther down the road, past

The big, rich homes of Bel Aire Beach,
You end up in a cornfield, and if you
Plunge into the green waves, walk the

Rows, you get lost in the cool shade,
Because the corn is good this year,
Ears big and thick as butter dishes.

If you sit in the cornfield, close your
Eyes, wait long enough, you can hear
The lonely, suspicious breathing of God.

Jazz Riff

A threatening breeze fans the lake. The
radio broadcasts severe tornado warn-
ings for Siouxland. Crickets scream.
The wind sings. Rips branches off trees,
hurls them into the lake. Big, sweeping
white caps clap against the point with
vicious whacks. Spray spits high in the
air. I can see the blue and white Amoco
sign down at the Marina, hear the buzz
of engines out on the lake; Evinrudes,
slick speedboats skipping over the
waves toward shore. Dance music from
the ballroom floats on the water. Time
dwells in my soul, and it seems if I died
the night would pick me up and levitate
me, suck my blood, play me like a rusty
flute. I open all my windows, lie down
on the floor and wait for the storm. The
bad weather slams in. Wind whistles
through my screen windows. Typed
pages whirl above me. They look like
giant moths. Hail pings the roof and the
demon wind howls like a wild coyote
hung up on barbed wire.

Gerry Mulligan Blues

Tuesday, a warm September day,
we were all hoping for an Indian
Summer--sun well into October
(the next day the temperature
dropped 60 degrees). This day
felt odd--like a new sweater.
A snap cracked--a whiplash--and
I knew this was a spark in my
brain, a boggling synapse that
would seriously change my life.
Frenchie LaRue warned me about
this one damp night in dark New
Orleans, but I didn't envision
such a scenario. You didn't
either, did you? But you've
heard the same sharp click in
your head, you've felt the ping
in your belly, and you knew it
was time to pay up and move on.

Navigating the Migration

Mallards circle the island
big ringnecks
a looping chain
swooping down on the lake
splashing safely, resting, sailing
like tin ducks in a shooting gallery

They're up again
winging low over the cornfield
near the shelterbelt
where Elmer Hanson waits
with his 16 gauge shotgun

The point duck takes a direct hit
stalls, falls, dives
two more are blasted out of the sky
feathers float to the lake
the rest of the flock scatters
chains up beyond the shelterbelt

It's war all the way south

Rewrite

It's graduation night and the high
school kids have built a leaping
bonfire down by the point.

I can hear them laughing, smell
charred weenies, see them outlined
down there, dark shadows against
the brilliant orange glow.

Two of them wander the shoreline.
I hear their soft voices in back
of my cabin, see them through the
window, watch them hold hands, kiss,
plot the future.

Nights like these loneliness curls
around me like tear gas. I sit in
the dark and wonder what happened
to that girl from Mississippi,
the one I knew back in college.

Nights like these time flees my
soul, sucked out by the shadows
on the dock, filling them with hope.

Nights like these I'd like to go
back, start over, slide one more time
out of that long, dark, evil tunnel.

Desperation

The drunk young men, the sweet young girls,
old men who suffer their happiness. Wives
whose husbands work the kill-floor. Waves
lap the shore, the slurping sound of sex. The
girls in the dorms. Women in the bars
downtown who long ago forgot the delicious
swoon of schoolgirl love. High school girls
watching videos. Old women alone in their
rooms reading novels. Music from the ball-
room on the point trebles across the lake.
Couples stroll the shoreline. The rustle of a
sweater. Her breasts shine like hot eyes in the
dappled moon-night. On the other side of the
lake, across from the packing plant, lonely
men hunch over the bar and gawk at strip-
pers. They spit dollar bills into their
G-strings. Cheap sex perfumed by popcorn
and stale beer. This night is an empty church
on Monday.

Thesis on Ending a Love Affair

When the woman yawns
her body bending, stretching
face grotesquely wrinkled
her mouth a lewd bazoo
sucking you deep into
her drowning boredom
you wonder what happened
to tight jeans, red sweaters
the pink impasto mouth
whip of the tongue

passion

it didn't last
never does
and the yawn
is your first clue
it's dead
this is when you
call the moving company

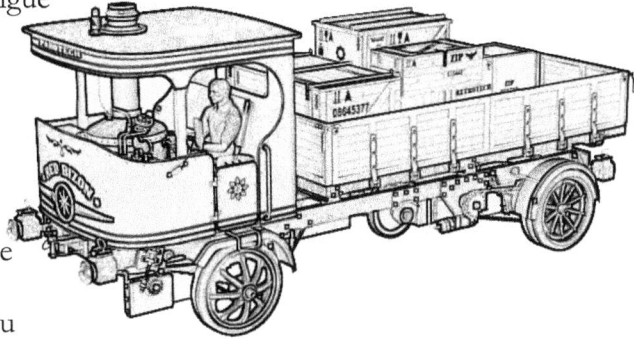

Harvest Time for the Grim Reaper

I smell Death...
It smells like the fever.
My nostrils reek with the stink.
I walk hand in hand with my
Sister Claudia, gathering
Sunflowers from the dirt packed
Prairie behind the little
Slatboard house that stands for
Home. Claudia doesn't smell Death.
She's running happily toward the
Banks of the Vermillion when it
Sneaks up and seduces her.
I stand helpless, watching Death
Give me my first taste of life.

Lakeshore Road

If you walk alone, a hot, dry
afternoon, just before the fall
harvest, when the corn is tall
and the stalks bend with fat ears,
the wind lifts husks from the field,
sails them across the road like
skeet. Near the spillway, little
boys hold a stringer of bullheads.
A dog sits in the dirt beside them,
tongue dripping hungry, head cocked
to the skewered fish. His tail
thumps, swats the ground. You see
these things. They become exaggerated,
glorified. Your mind burns them into
a masterpiece as you sit on the edge
of the spillway and listen to the
roar of the lake pour over the mossy
cement, watch the pike, perch, carp,
crappie, blue gill, plunge out of the
lake, splash in the foamy swirl below;
trapped, sentenced forever to the dry,
cracked, creek beds south of the county
line. They fight frantically, try and
jump back into the lake, wiggle, slap
at the slick wall. They leap, spin,
fall, smash down on jagged rocks.
They bleed. You can sit and watch
the fish give in, swim away defeated,
and you can hear the harsh caw of a
crow overhead, see a wrinkled corn husk
drift by, feel the heat of the sun, taste
the fear of death.

Dirty Trick

Hot September days press in, a swiftly moving storm, a black wall of bad memories. You recall when you were 13, the day your brother died--you sat on the curb in front of the pool hall with your ball glove, spitting in the pocket, rubbing, punching the leather, waiting for news from the Madison Hospital. You needed this brother. You had already lost a sister to the steaming Midwest fever. You sat there and saw the big, black Lincoln swing off Highway 34. It crawled down Main Street. It was your crazy, drunken aunt, the one who owned the beer joint out on the Norwegian Gravel. She pulled up at the curb and told you your brother didn't make it, said she had him in the back. You saw the tiny pine box on the seat, the clutter--the empty whiskey bottles, smashed cigarette packs, and torn, blue panties, a crusted Kotex. She said she was taking your brother up to Willoughby's Funeral Home for fixing. You wanted to kill this woman, but you backed up, turned and ran to the softball field where they were choosing sides for a game. They took you for right field. You jogged out into the weedy pasture, stood alone, pulled the bill of your cap low, and wiped away the tears with the thumb of your glove.

Walking Under Water

There was a drowning
In the lake today.
A young boy fell out

Of a fishing boat.
He went down like a
Sinker. His friends

Dived for him, but gave
Up and called in a
Dragging operation

From the county. They
Used metal scoops and
Big, dry catch nets.

I saw all this from
My dock where I sat
reading poetry, sipping

Jack Daniels. I had
Questions: Was it a
Warm death? What's the
Last thing he saw? His
Friends, the sky, my
Cabin, me, hell, God?

They dragged late,
Brought him up all
Purple and bloated.

The boats, the crowd,
The gawking humanimals,
Have all gone home now,

And a slice of setting
Sun reflects an orange
Flame licking the water.

I can smell a fresh kill
From the packing plant,
Pungent, sweet, gagging

Smoke hangs in the hot,
Humid summertime. A fish
Jumps out of the lake

Next to my dock and knifes
Back into the slick surface
With a sick, sucking sound.

The Sacred Circle

A year of reconciliation
The governor said so
But Wounded Knee still bleeds

Wind from hell
Temperature 28 below
The Great Plains an ice rink

They rode from Bullhead
South across the Cheyenne
Down through the Badlands
Onto the Pine Ridge

Half of them quit

It was a matter of timing

But the clock cannot weep
Its heart is frozen

Bad Night in the Badlands

The night breathes
A gravel road yawns
Stray dogs gather

The night whispers
Antelopes dart for cover
Moonlight sprays the hills

The night moans
A mallard honks back
Shadows in a gully

The night howls
Someone kicks the bucket
Church bells ring

The night screams
Lightning zaps the sky
Death dances in the wind

Down the road
In the Black Hills
An Indian prays

Requiem for Religion

Brian Williams narrates a story about millions
dying of hunger in Africa. Outside a driving
rain drills the slick lake like rifle bullets.

A truck shifts down in front of my cabin and
sprays gravel in the ditch. Cracks of light
illuminate the sky. The wind howls, picks up,

pushes lush, thick, weeping waves against the
shore. A jet roars overhead. Thunder booms
in counterpoint. I peer out my window. Bright

electric flashes light up the dock, make it
look like a wet stick of chewing gum. Cool
breezes whistle off the lake; sweet smell of

fresh dirt. More lightning. Flashbulb bright.
Hospital white. The island beyond the dock
looks like a ship stuck in time. A squirrel

leaps from a tree, scoots across the top of my
backyard fence, disappears. This is early fall,
the first blush of orange. The whitecaps foam,

the wind rips leaves from the trees. A black
thunderhead drapes the top of a silo across
the lake. The rain drums my roof. A knock taps

the front door. It's two young men with the
Mormon Church. They're soaking, hair slick
and matted. They offer me literature and ask

to talk. I invite them in and fix coffee. They
disapprove when I light a cigarette and pour a
shot of Jack Daniels in my cup. They ask if I've

read the Book of Mormon. I haven't. They tell

me about it. The squirrel is back. He sits on
the window ledge and stares at the Mormons.

He puts his paws on the screen and scratches.
The TV blares a story about a man who walks
into a Catholic church and shoots a praying

priest. The thunder bellows--low, thick rumbles,
the rain slashes faster, harder, turns to hail,
pelts my cabin like thousands of falling rocks.

Servant of the Truth

The truculent pup
that belonged to the
couple in the brown cabin
started all the trouble

A cool fall day and I'd been
holed up in my room reading
Soren Kierkegaard's Diary
the part where he says
the thinker or poet
who forms an opinion
will never be popular
not because they're difficult
but because it demands quiet
hours working with the mind
intimate knowledge of yourself
and insolation

Just like Kierkegaard
I needed excitement
of creative work
to help me forget
life's brutal trivialities
the endless, boring repetition

That's why I stayed
in my cabin
reading, writing, clinging
to the drapes
that's why people think I'm crazy

I decided to take a hike
get some exercise, do some thinking.

I walked the cobblestone curve
around the lake, sniffed
the rich, crisp bonfires,

watched autumn leaves
roll a lazy turn,
said to the ground
a rusty, crusty carpet

Nelson's Bait Shop advertised
fat minnows and fresh nightcrawlers
and the spillway gushed water over
a rock waterfall, the spray
tumbling into a pool of swirling
foam and bubbles

I walked by the brown cabin
and spotted bulldog leaped
from the porch
growled and clawed dirt

Dogs offend my sensibilities
they have no right
shitting on lawns
humping human's legs
barking, snipping, intimidating
pedestrians.

I challenged Spot
threw up my fists
flashed a couple wicked
left-right combinations

This confused the poor beast
he scratched deeper into the dirt
the corner of his mouth curled
like burning paper

A little fat boy who resembled
the fat kid in the beanie from
the *Little Rascals* rushed out
to the lawn and eyeballed
the dog and me

Spot pawed a clump of grass
I waited
the fat kid watched
Spot parked
I barked back
Spot leaped

my timing was perfect (life is timing)
I nailed him with a right cross
flush to the snoot

He dropped to the sidewalk
like a sack of marbles
One, two, three, four, five, six

Spot was up on five
he backed off, shook his head

The kid ran into the house screaming
Ma! He's beating up Happy!

The ugly child's mother stumbled
out the door of the cabin
She belched and said: *Did you
hit our dog?*

She had on a frizzy red robe
her face was blotched alcohol pink
her hair matted and spindled
against her sweaty forehead
she wore red slippers
with pink puff balls on the toes

I yelled: *Back off you wench!*
The dog snarled
I danced
he circled
I bobbed and weaved
he barked
I barked back

he pounced
I socked him with a solid left

The woman shrieked: *Oh my God!*
you hit Happy. Oh, Jesus!
You're beating up our dog!

I went into the mandatory
eight count for Happy
he was dazed
he lay on his side gasping
his spotted, black body heaving
huffing and puffing
one eye walleyed me

The woman attacked me
pounded her fists on my chest
How could you do this?
How could you hit Happy?
You fiend!

I beg your pardon, Madam,
I was merely mixing metaphors!

Her eyes were beady, bloodshot
spit flew from her mouth
she wrestled me to the ground
squirmed around on top me
I got a hard-on
it thumped against her leg.

She gasped: *You pervert!*

I rolled over and pinned
the woman beneath me
my cock slapped at her
like a perch in a gunny sack

The little fat boy jumped on

hammered at my back and shouted:
You hit Happy! You hit Happy!

Happy lay dazed on his side
next to us
that one eye still on me

I flipped Fatty
he did a somersault and belly flopped
I twisted away from the vile woman
got up and jogged away

The woman and the fat boy chased me
throwing rocks, hollering, yelping
about Happy

As Kierkegaard before me
I believe I owe it to
the beastiality of the times

Life would have been the same for me
in any other century

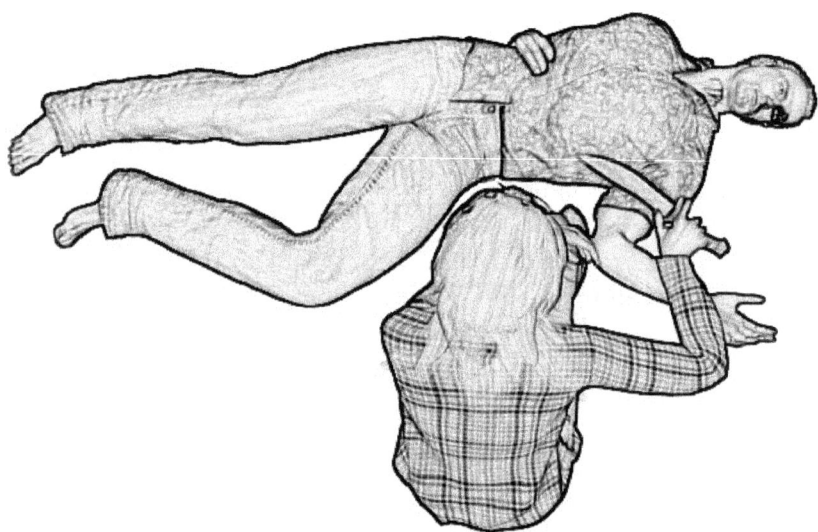

Cameron Steele
Attribution

According to women, when to use knives

Women got to know when to use knives, when to slip metal
through their common-law men, metal words will do, but knives
work best sometimes when he come home too late, too wet,
those beggar eyes, yes, slippery lips, he speaking without words
clutching house keys, glass bottle against thigh and groin,
she in her tee-shirt, common and cold, and clutching at -- what?

What newspapers leave out.

What I got? Always women want to know, words clicking down throats,
snapped off by sore molars, 3 a.m. cigarettes, cigars if he left them.
If he did, when he come home, he call her baby -- thief -- bitch --
close them wolf-eyes, men always do; didn't he get worlds,
life with a girl who smile when she told, when she ain't,
she stay with him when bud's got him against walls and the law
What I got but a man? She knows. Left without words
and his words without love and too late but that's

What newspapers leave out.

Woman in kitchen, man is dead.
Morning headlines a day or two, three later.
The official report, they say they got, and her mug
shot: Wide, dog eyes, cigarette lips.
Woman of women who know what they got, words
refuse to forget: On slippery nights they cure what common cold.

What newspapers leave out.

Dreaming of ducks

She flies on prairie winds, sifts through purple sloughs
of memory, finds her father. Hip-waders and hunter's cap,
he ploughs through milk-grass. She watches with dream lashes:
the youth of him gleams like lead in barrels of South Dakota shotguns.
She watches him – his nose a red beak, blue heat in his eyes -
the ducks don't fly today, she reads in green sky, diluted warmth of air.

As a baby, her first word – duck – she said to yellowed farm air,
Charles City, east coast, Virginia Muck and the Cows that slewed
slowly through dead purple cornfields as DaDa crows "I'm
gonnagityew damned cows, yessir, I'm gonnaputta cap
inyerhead, helpme God," and help God when the gun
comes out, jabbing that jaundiced sky, whiplashes

of metal at Cows in violet cornfields. They don't bat lashes,
just mosey through life. At 12, the girl stands straight in salt air
at the Bay-house summer dock. Dad steadies her and BB gun,
whispers "Yes!Yes!" behind tousled slews
of curls beneath her dirty Chesapeake Bay cap.
Her neck-skin calms beneath gray eyes.

Still, she squeals, sucks in sea-salt, eyes
the glass bottle at the dock's end through blonde lashes.
She tugs the trigger, hears the tckCAP!
of the BB cracking water, salt pieces of air
but misses the damn bottle. "Yes!Yes! Yer boundfertha slews
of South Dakota!" He smiles at the gun.

When she packs to leave, at 18, she finds a BB gun,
cased away, dust-covered – the left-over hands, eyes
of attic life. "Yes! Yes!" she laughs, dusting away slews

of cobwebs from attic windows, finds her father's dark eyelashes:
black and sweet and focused in leaves of Richmond Fall Air.
He packs her trunk, dreams tucked safe beneath South Dakota cap.

In her dreams, western Virginia Mountains prick her mind, cap
nightmares of lonely, busy, black days – all school but no gun
lessons, no flying ducks. Now Cows mosey through lilac air

broken by hills. Not the deep prairies of his South Dakota eyes.
She walks with books, lives without "Yes!Yes!" sleeps in lashes
of midday light. In the yellowest afternoons, dreams send her to
sloughs.

She watches a wind-butted Hunter's cap, Dakota blue eyes.
His Virginia red hands, the brown-battered shot-gun, all through
day-dream lashes.
And don't ducks fly together? In slews, through prairie winds to
mountain air.

Revelation

Sometimes, in breaking, waking life,
it's easy to feel what you are a
22 nearly 23-year-old girl
She tries to become a woman each morning
on her own
all by herself, she sends off rent checks, fixes leftovers
for lunch, dresses in hand-me-down blazers
thanks God shoulder-pads are back in style (sort-of)
and stubs her toe on the crumbled brick
of her duplex.
Spinning through long hours of nine to six-thirty work:
Papers, phone calls from sources (of what, she wonders), left-over lunches
and readers whose pulses she's supposed to have fingers on.
Work but still it pays little
for rent checks and gives her far less time to look
up at the sky
when it changes.
It's easy to feel what you fear you will become a
girl caught hopelessly in the path of words
others have already blazed.

And catching her breath,
she will finally sit down
one night
on those broken bricks.
She'll look up past the dimming eve,
and the blinking red dot on top of the radio tower.
Through clean air (kind of) and faint stars.

And waking, she finds
for the first time
the crooked handle of the big dipper, breaking
the night above her duplex
into what she has been
and all that's left for becoming.

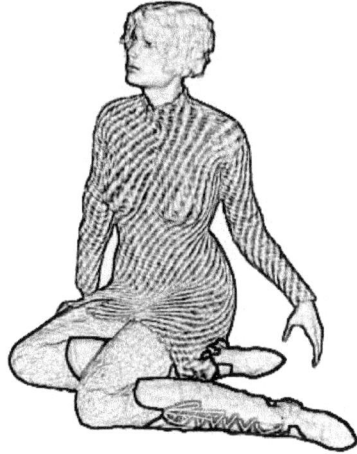

Orogenesis

Arch your back
and push your body
up on weak wrists
slender fingers
hips widening out
to the world.
Can you sustain
this infinite gesture
of what which is welcome
of that which is yet to come?
Isn't it magic?
The heart thrums
like an ancient drum
along the insides
of sweaty thighs.
This is orogenesis:
The folding of yourself
into the shape of every woman
and every one
who is breathing.

The Bagley Road goat

Horace Gowan for years
lived near the crook
or bend, some called it,
in Bagley Road.
The Bend in Bagley Road:
where Gowan kept a goat
and one one-eyed llama.

But the goat –
her pewter penny eyes,
knotted legs,
lovely mews bawling out
across the loam and dirt and ponds,
soft tongue on octogenarian knuckles
– the goat Gowan loved.

One October morning
frost or cool ghosts bent Gowan's knees
like Bagley Road.
The old, beaky man was slow to rise.
He fingered hard snot around raw nostrils,
slurped cold medicine,
and stopped cold at this:

Goat Marigold whinnying
like a mare. She cried from the
back Bagley loblollies as
Gowan prayed for a sore leg
or deep hunger, (the greedy goat!),
running through his rolling yard.

But Horace, wise and old, knew prayers often
went awry, crooked as his fingers
or bent lanes where old men lived.

That night Gowan dreamed:
rough tongues, bloody throats, dead goats
and the neighbor's pit-bull
barking up the bend in Bagley Road.

Shale barren sestina

They climb in sweat and winds through mountain shale,
rocks crumbling, faint rattles of imagined snakes sound in wary
eyes - *Do you hear that?* Whispers, climbing and halting near
buckwheat, wild in arid flakes of Virginia shale barrens. And here
– kate's mountain clover soft, unabashed next to hiking
boots. *They see you, they see you.* They see - hairs white, fuzz-armor
to protect from sun-gods green veins of leaves.

They reach for endemic things, noting *ipsothermic, Climatis
albicoma* leaves net-veined in notebooks pressed against knees and
bellies and rocks in suns of shale barrens. *kurlink-! klink!* echoes
broken mountains in seas of wind-gods, chuffing through
stunted *Pinus virginiana,* eyeing amateur biogeographers stumble
up, up through clovered slopes. *They see you. They see* – Virginia in
lines of floral tubes wild

against backdrops of barren hills. Their hearts wilding around
the edges, syncing with distant hiss of rattles in leaves. They are
humans on south-facing slopes, they see in clovers white and
green and Kate's own. *Can you hear* – the rocks speaking, They
whisper, they listen: pitted voices, mountain eyes. There is
something living here. In this place, these shale seas

of Virginia Appalachia. They trace back through leatherflower,
see pearl-petals against gray *clicking* crumbs of barren
wilderness? They are human – but on hills they move slowly
down, no more *I* – just quiet of place and wind-songs through
gap-toothed leaves. What god can exist if not through life on
broken, breaking rocks? What woman knows love without first
feeling mountain-clovered

dreams? In this place they know something about clovers. They
stand at bottoms of Blue Ridge metashales, seeing up into
something known, illusive. What rocky shores life can heave
towards skies. *They see you, wild and good.* They have hearts shaped
– now – like leaves. There is singing through yellow buckwheat
to eyes

of hidden rattlesnakes. In their minds, they know *I* – as shaled Virginia mountains. They feel life through clovers. Radiance in cordate, palmate, pinnate leaves, *they are leaving you, Climatis albicoma,* see backpacks and boots and see them on wheels leaving. But *can you hear* - whispers, wild in humans. They cannot forget your sweet life on rocks.

There is something filled in human eyes to see barren lands of life, wild in buckwheats, clovers, and *they know you* shale rocks flowing through human veins

Serious sestina

I never used words like true and love
in the same sentence or accurate way.
On scalding mornings or steeped noons
or after drinks at some bar, I'd sway
to the songs in my head; making room
for lies and blinking eyes to some boy

or man I knew I should need. But boy
I didn't know a damn thing about loving
with fingers and teeth and world-filled rooms.
How can you learn about cotton sheets? The way
they become some kind of cool skin, the sway-
backed girl I've always been in the afternoon

changes to a thing straighter. I am nooning
with you, the spring-summer infinite boy
I sought in spheres of early-hour swaying.
Remember Gaia was strong, loved
only what she could make in her own way.
Didn't need no thing, no man, no bedroom

to be wrapped in cool cotton. Rooms
fill my head when – just like that – it's noon
and my legs are words I never knew; ways
I wouldn't take 'til you, the boy
who gives me a sky wrought with some love
that earth-woman won't ever reach. Sway

with me. Build me into a mountain swaying
with hips and lips cuz I will give you room
to become a God or the First Man I love
or sentences strung out like afternoons
laced with something wilder. My sweet boy,
am I saying it clear? I have weighed

it all out, rolled across the minutes and ways
a woman forgets what she thought she knew; is swayed
by the slightest glance from a man now a boy
in her hands and eyes and spines. The world is roomy
and bigger than skies and oceans in afternoon
mythology when I'm steeped in your love.

Boy, this is it: I got the words and the way
to love you true (I don't blink). With you, I'll sway
through time and noons and cotton bedrooms.

Leaving love in spring

It's easy to say
been down this road before,
walked beneath willows
knowing the way winged gods
can take from you
lips
legs
life as trees in flight, in love.

What did I lose?
Not conviction or pretty baubles
or vines.
Never sanity
ever the loops of it drowse
in some seedy April pond.

You left poppies in my ears – catkins
rawing my throat.

I have lost this:
How to speak without bark.
And when I run fingers across
some man's forearm, this:
that green wind rifling between thighs
slaking what thirst.

It's easy to see this old road,
the way without branches in wind.

God,

I am tired of writing about dead people
and their mothers who are always
praying to you, asking their sons, husbands, daughters, cousins
not be dead
but just gone somewhere
for a little while -- for barbecue in Birmingham
or maybe to Atlanta for a key bump
and a fist.
Yes, these mothers are always praying, we can
handle lies and disappointment and white lines
but not death, never.

Once I could look at dead the way I was supposed to:
as a headline, using verbs like "allege" and plenty of attribution
from cops.
But, God, I am tired.
This weekend, after I felt the last mother
turn into a fish on the phone when I asked:
When did they tell you he was murdered?

I realized I want Anthony's job in Faith
or Nick in Sports
or Lisa with her columns on the seasons.
Do you ever feel this way, when mothers
are gutted and splayed on a cleaning station before you,
when they, even for a moment, stop praying?

Freestyle

It's safer here
quiet and shimmery.
Couldn't you be a fish or whale
or some underwater mammal
that doesn't sweat or cry
or feel the pounding of some male hand,
the weight of that whole big solid world?
It hurts underwater, too.
But you feel shiny
strong and tendony;
the stretch of fingertips
pelvis
quick pulsing toes and thighs.
Currents are more natural than air.
It's worse when you break
concentration —
force the head sideways
under armpit and breathe.
In those seconds
you miss the black T on the bottom
silent unwavering unbroken movement.

Feel the heat of those eyes.
Wretched whistling
from the man you must please.
That mammally skin,
the weight of nights
unnatural
dull, the hours of it.
Swim on, little fish.
The race isn't
the sisters in lanes beside you.

They matter less than the dry,
dangerous place above –
where weakness is a virtue
Sound a promise.
Gravity the punishment of man.

Thoughts, for a second?

Oh and you were a boy then
blue eyed and I watched
every morning the world
play across your armhairs.
Maybe we could have ended
there in that bed after twenty
embraces and drink-laced
words;
instead of charting sober, lovely
courses together.
Now what I see on
the dawns when you still
sleep:
It's not the earth
or dirt
or a boy with eyes.
It's time passing;
fluted with flesh
that feels so much like my own.

Casualties of nature

We lost them —
the holding hands
bodies
dancing
long hours in the yard
cool evenings on the porch
quoting from favorite
Western shows
and *La Vie En Rose*.

We lost the smells
of the house
warm and woodsy
Bill hewing some
fencepost
in the shed
Linda smoking a pipe
tapping her foot
along to hidden rhythms
an Edith Piaf record.

And it was —
on the porch
in the house
all over the yards —
La Vie En Rose.
Life's pits and stems
cast against our parents
magic.

The storm came in April.
Hold me close
Linda said.
Hold me fast.

The humming of the earth
opening up.

No one told them —
When heaven sighs,
it yawns with teeth
snapped limbs
stinking debris
looped around
the air.

We found them
in woods
next to the yard.
Every bone in Bill's
body broken –
this rough-hewn man
holding hands
with the woman
who spoke French
and smoked tobacco
from pipes.

We lost the way
every word
every day
turned into songs.

How easy they became
art. How easy they
made falling in love
with routine
and dancing next to
a wooden, sagging front door.

Dear Mom

It was easy to write this,
pictures of you spinning
through my lashes
on the last starless night in March:

You rounding leaves into a blue tarp,
one Wellshire Fall and you
serene, still on a winter pew - how silently,
Holy those Christmas Eves were
in barely-filled sanctuaries.
You and the kitchen mornings, thumb in mouth
thin ponytail capped against your neck...
August evenings freckled you,
working puzzle pieces through fingers.

Tonight, the hard, flat swing beneath
my thighs and the velvet letters
darker than air.
I'm writing to say I'm not lost
or old and sad like those ladies on TV.
Maybe alone
maybe tired and sometimes scared,
the way you were when I first became.
but this is no SOS, no message
just a bottle of words
saying yes, I love you,
and the twisting, circling thoughts of why
I always will.

The Arson

The brick house with the metal roof is no
longer breathing.
The home bowed then folded in on itself
this morning
red then dead
around five
after ten years
but really it started to die yesterday morning
around nine
before school when mom and dad
spoke with lips that didn't really move at all
what do you do with that?
and now mom and dad are weeping in the
winter yard because
again,
they ask bitter air,
how do you explain something that breathes
and breathes and breathes
until one morning it is not alive
just moving smoke?
who took it from us, who grinned
red and dead
and our children were still dancing
they ate cereal in that blackened
spot
just yesterday before
even then they
were still dreaming
sweetly
beneath that metal roof.

Chief, tell us where does the smoke go?
and the sun's rising in that steel sky
we are watching them run toward the open
door

and the black stairs
the foyer which buckled but never burned
until now
or yesterday
and they are touching the soot of our family picture
and this is what we see:
the brick house is so damn dead
but mom and dad they have arms
and legs and kissing mouths
red and sweaty in January.

Following your lies:

I am not a cuddly person.
And everyone can see my eyes fisting and closed
when you are around.
I don't need any part of you:
Not your tongue on my face
or arms around my scarred belly.
Sometimes my body is a tree
or a horse broken by hail and hours.
And sometimes I don't know
how to take punches from a glance.

    What you really say
    you say through half-open lashes
    when you think
    no one's looking, especially not me:

Want me. Love me. Lead me.

Tell It Like It Is

"I don't dance,"
he mutters, a napkin
covering
his sharp chin.
Under the thin table cloth,
both knees are bouncing.

Upon the dying mare

He will pull her slackened snout
wet as it is
into his lap and weep.
The many mornings

and moons
he found his calves
hitched against her breathing flanks
as they picked paths along the Concho.

And the San Angelo nights he twisted
his thumbs through her knotted hair –
he thinks, prolly knows, if he lets himself
turn over those mudstones bottoming out his stomach –
he should of never slept.

Calm as the stars, she was, but
he still shouldn't of let the weather of sore bones
sand over his eyes, even for a second,
in that gaping, gypsum eve.

All it takes is some streaky thing
a rush of rain or a pop
of some dumb guy with an old gun,
and her skittish nerves will open
some road the boy can't take.
Just something like that.

He will miss her shelter,
her blood slick, thick
and animal as his own.
He rolls away the river for her grave.

He weeps.

Barbara Duffey
The Verge of Thirst

Texas

Aubade with a Quincy Jones Biography on PBS
In response to Pound's "The Garret"

Dawn came in like Philip Marlowe
drunk on rye and gray with stubble.
You called in sick and I took you

to the pharmacy. Michael asked,
"How's your wife?" ringing up your drugs.
You've never told him that I'm not

your wife. The Texas Family Code,
line 2.401, declares
we're married if we represent

to others that we're married (check),
we live together (check), and we
agree to be married.

Between aneurysms, Quincy
and his girlfriend from the *Mod Squad*
married so she'd gain legal rights

to his remains, her grip of him
wouldn't cremate in the L.A.
County Morgue. Come, let us pity

the married and the unmarried.
He didn't die either time, but
I turn from the TV to look

at dear you, neither my husband nor
my unhusband, eyes glazed over
like cakes.

I dole your dose and brew your tea.
Yes, life has something better than this
hour of waking together: this power

To guarantee your body lies
With me till I say otherwise.

I Run Errands by Myself

We ate the extra-fancy
star-krimson pears. Your
clothes fill the boxes.

In the pharmacy,
aftershave without your cheek.
I flip up the cap.

I bought your brand of toothpaste
so my mouth would taste
as if I'd kissed you.

Goodwill—I donate
the boxes, all your freckles,
and the telephone.

At home, the sound of pear skin
peeled into the disposal.

Summer Night, Houston

I sweeten the air toasting coconut for my icebox pie.

Thermodynamics is the study of the transience of temperature.

I stand in the glow of the oven, lit so I can watch the flakes brown and warm the crooks of my knees while I read a book: a physicist in love with a woman named Opal.

The heat feels like your tongue, most exciting where I'm most open.

The starlet on the TV talk show wears a floor-length, long-sleeved black gown so no one can see her bones.

The whistle of the 12 o'clock Union Pacific quiets the distance between where I live and what I can know.

Doppler proposed his effect in the work "On the Coloured Light of the Binary Stars and Some Other Stars of the Heavens."

The host and actress have both been made into dolls, and the host says his is too shy to hold her doll's hand.

Neither the physicist nor Opal has been in love before.

My question for you hangs out of reach on the oven's heat.

We Can Definitively Report that We Have Not Released Man-Eating Badgers in the Vicinity

Mavericks per the law of fur and claw, they sing their call sign, "Only When Provoked." And boy, are you One to Provoke, you who went to the vet in the flash-flood warning, knowing you'd be stranded, just to buy prescription cat food. You'd stroke a badger's coat, coax it down from my bureau, rub its face beside its croc-strong jaw. What do you expect? You heard the man—no one else is responsible. Just you, you and your fatal kindness, leaving me alone.

How to Bake the Famed Cushion Cake, Requisite for Bridal Showers and a Favorite of Our Staff

—after the *Betty Crocker Picture Cook Book,* 1950

A diamond like a pill
crouches in the scale's cup—
its weight just that

of starling skull, of eyelid,
of twine to truss the turkey—
waiting to be set, bedeck me.

Meanwhile, I bake, heed: *Measure*
as exactly as a druggist.
For the cake to rise, balance

one thumb baking soda,
a belt loop baking powder,
two fists sifted flour:

Level flour with your
knife's spine, drawn across
the top as if plowing

snow off steel. The cushion cake
plumps when baked, forms
a hollow core to stuff with

down and vow. The Egyptians,
weighing hearts and feathers,
call to pit my heart

against your diamond.
If my heart is lighter,
I'll be yours. You'll

dispense me. Otherwise,
I'll knife out doses
of Valium for those

who bake their cakes
with heaping cupfuls, flatten them
to heavy discus hearts.

Combo, Per the Norm

Torrents bewitch the Aswan, hew its arc
as it kisses them. I am a crack
in the thermal, one bark from panic, an elk
on an icecap when I wade into eros,
but I adore you, my net, as you grab
—ahem——my ticklish knee and market your
deal until I agree on the sale
and nod at your sweet menace. A swami
once said that da Vinci would never reach
his acme since the rarest pig rose
in the smoke from the censer, but eras
wiggle past with no sign of lending him
their obscurity. Ah, so the scorepad
stands against predestination, fortunes
all shown to be skits in the Big Apple.
Eos breaks on our bed, on the labs
that show just how much is left to chance, love.
No need to nag, poke, or plan: Let's occur.

Scabies

They burrowed an architecture into my skin and planted their eggs,
whose yolks fed fire
to their growing young. They painted the ceilings with flying cacti
and Harley Davidson logos and their mite-angels, round like
pufferfish,
with four pairs of filamentous legs, two crab-like pinchers and
wings.

The scabies set up easels on the floors, and each easel foot
scorched the skin beneath,
which began to smoke and peel, in layers like phyllo dough, and it
puffed in welts.
I was allergic to my own bones, they wanted to unmoor
themselves,
they were chafing against my rhubarb muscles.

The scabies rode their motorcycles down my veins; I scratched,
caused accidents,
the greatest of which was the subject for an epic painting entitled
"Babs's Left Elbow,"
in which my right hand featured prominently as the agent of doom.

I applied Lindane, an insecticide so poisonous it was banned from
use in farmers' fields.
The colony scorched, they fell down dead in their dens, and my
body
dissolved them like salt in water. I was then cured of art.

How Simple Machines Work

You will never get more energy out of a system than you put into it.
You will never get as much energy out of a system as you put into it.
           — Utah State University Junior Engineering
Workshop

Rain on a neighbor's shutters, the sound of
learning someone else is pregnant. About

the air, it hung loose as a pinafore,
a thumbed pocket with a grain inside. When

the moon was white as my pall and dog-chained
to dry land, it seemed easier to pitch

my tent alone than bind my body to
you, spoiler pitman, and your paper ribs,

your steam-engine muscle, your Rube Goldberg
romance. But when I maroon my mule self

you always winch me back, even though you
lose heat to friction every time the rope
rubs against the spool as it's wound and wound.

Lauds

Praise to the air so choked in smoggy sheath
each streetlamp halos rainbows around it,
and praise to running hard, its raw-throat breath,
sweat glistening my hairline edged in grit.
Praise to the gravel mine that cut faces
of red rock from the scrub oak on the hill
we can see from the front window—snow laces
a ground of iron. Praise to my love's will,
because my own is not enough to keep
the collection agencies away. I
don't know how to dust or mop or sweep
or use the stove for anything but pie,
but cross-section any piece of middling
stuff dirty brown like me—I'll make it sing.

Andy Aria

Ursa Major turns on a peg—that neon
opal—to shine above our motor home
with a saber's leggy élan. You stole
much ado from her on our watery
dates, when you put my heart in a ewer
and poured it back into my jawed gown. You
still tempt me, knead me, reel me in with
sake and tales, and the fleeing ease of
the highway unites us outside each
city's gate—Boise mocks us with her
tassels of streetlights joshing in the rear-view.
On my behalf please open up your clasped
woe, sore pea in your lame wrist, as around us
the powerlines twang out a bass-clef loss.

Wheel & Axle

We did nothing on a whim. The friction
of the multiplying moment pulled my
guide, my wagon, to a stream of thimble-
tears until he took my hand and kissed me
when bidden. Love had winched us in from the
wet swarf ground out by the rack-and-pinion
planet, so here we were in front of the
nave and the assembly. We had been clods
in the differential, and now we were
driving an axis of belly and nose.
Aren't we all just hubs housing helical
slave drivers? We wanted our gyroscope
spinning out like a spur-wheel on track,
our little linch-pin, as soon as possible.

Cento: "Instinct," by Lester Del Rey

The old brain in his chest even seemed
to think better now. It was good to have
a new body. A good body. How good
it was to be alive and to be a
robot. But the old worries: They were no
nearer re-creating Man than they had
been when they started. They began dissecting
the body of the female failure,
the reason behind the lack of success.
How well do you know your history?
I mean about the beginning

After Our Talk

The sky, mauve from particulates—pollution,
precipitation—purples to the horizon.

On the radio, Kevin Mahogany sings, *It's so lonesome
in the evening when the sun goes down.*

The sidewalk's graffitied "feel better"
faces away from my window.

I sleep it off.

We dine at the Chinese restaurant I loved as a kid.

I wake; new snow
articulates each branch.

From the lit windows, started cars, energetic
shoveling, it's clear that everyone else
has heeded the sidewalk's suggestion.

The houses and their blue addresses, tinged with
dawn, blush at the weatherman's "It's snowing
down south"—girlcode for "your slip is showing."

The close gray sky admits nothing.

Who made the footprints beside
the dog tracks in the snow? I envy him.

I thought I'd told you correctly.

Tele, from afar; *phone*, sound:
Even etymology reminds me
I'm off.

I had to read the Winter Safety E-mail
to know how to step from my car onto ice.

I've been told my slips are telling,
that black ice is clearer than speech.

South Dakota

Summer Weather

        They push back the thunderstorm time. The west's
warm wind gathers elsewhere. First, blue elbows
        through the clouds, and then is squelched, the sky is

      just the color of bright. When I look up,
I've opened my eyes to mid-day light when
        I'd gone to sleep in the pitch black, it's that

      dramatic in its wash over the street,
the white light crisping everything. I can't
        take pictures on a day like today when

      the colors aren't themselves having cleaned up
for visitors and inside I'm just so
        angry. In some ways, my life has turned out

      the way I wanted, but the others grate
on my patience, especially on days
        stark like today when I can't look away.

Bloom: South Dakota

after Jack Spicer

I.

The geese stood still in the sky while I
was yanked south by spring, abruptly like
a roller-coaster carriage taking
track up my own driveway. Their honking
dopplered off, left me with the scrim
of snow against garages all
along the alley, tufted from
inertia as we, weathered, halted.

II.

I'm worried about the oak. The others on the block have leafed
out, budded out, sent green branches into the oblivion of the over-
sidewalk air. The grass seeds, the daffodils
hazard, our oak, in "winter condition," winters
       on on the road verge. The ghosts of the across-the-street
       oak stumps paint pink dots on live oaks in jest.
Or jealousy, the envy of life. I have lived my life full of envy. I
ignore Rilke. I won't change. The seasons are the seasons, nothing
more, no metaphor but what we've made.

III.

The spirea blooms
fall around the neighbor's porch.
fall on the sidewalk and fall on
the grass.
fall on baby
rabbits and on black squirrels and on certain
small birds, maybe
finches.
fall in the wind, whisked across
the grass.

droop but never fall.
dangle on the branches' stooped curve.
fall on nothing, on the bit before the air.
hide since spring is late.
fall across your carriage—no, that's a lie, fall across
you when I hid you in the shrubbery. You tracked them
in the carriage by yourself, later, after your rescue.
and the blooms bloom, so mindless, so obviously, so
stupidly, so compactly when a noun is its own verb. I envy it.

IV.

The neighbor sprays our dandelions
surreptitiously. Nothing pins our grass
with pricks of color, there is nowhere an
absence of green. Our lawn is in his seed-
space, in the air commuting to his air.
We share an armrest in the theater
of Sixth Avenue. He reaches over,
straightens our tie, whisks crumbs off our lapel.
Meanwhile, the seed heads down the street spin
into the May twilight oblivion.

V.

This is the story of a red-winged blackbird. At
first, it lived by the Missouri, like Lewis &
Clark. Then, it moved from water, on the verge
of thirst. A puddle, a breakwater, a stock dam.
A line of wetlands north to shallow lakes.   A nest
on Firesteel Creek, a mate from the trees in
the shelterbelt on Foster Avenue. It was
a place where you could hatch your eggs, a place where you
could feed someone a worm, a place where you could molt,
just enough moisture to keep your throat loud.

VI.

The loam lush, over-
damp, planting so late
it was in the news.
The remote-controlled
tractors turn furrows

computer-programmed
in the background of
the front-page photo.
My office-mate's son
comes home from college
early, an A.S.,
since State's software's old.
It sends a row of
ghost tillers down troughs
of fertile earth dark
as infertile hell.

VII.

The neighbors roto-till their backyard garden, all the squash sprouts
green the rows. The farmers past the city line will have to
ensile all the extra, there's just so, so much, and the cows
can only eat so much.

VIII.

All winter I wondered
about the upside-down
buckets behind Carol's
fence line, and when she turned
them over, the roses
underneath leafed out and
bloomed, their petals pink dots
between the rows of squash.

IX.

The lilac bloomed just one
week this year, the purple
whisked westward on June winds,
my emissary to
any outside world that
might need proof I had grown
something, something that lived.

Someone Asks

about my greatest
insecurity; maybe
we're playing an
icebreaker, maybe
we got too quickly

drunk at the party,
but I'm having a hard time
deciding—would it be worse
to not be smart, or to be
a bad parent? And I don't mean

not optimal, I mean
fatal, a diaphragm
of plastic across
his windpipe,
a slip head-first

off the changing table,
a thump against the wall
in the middle of the night
when he won't stop crying.
Everyone could say,

"You would never do
such a thing," but the news
is full of just such things and
the parents who do them,
and then jump out the window

of the burning apartment
onto the frost-hardened
backyard. What if I had
just one drink too many,
the threshold between my

imagination and my actions
worn down so that I tumbled over
just that once? The difference between
me and the parents on the news—just
the price of our alcohol? I put my hope

in my overuse of this word "just"—
if I know the level of the threshold's
lip, I can preserve it,
hold that little dancing body
until I die first.

Diesel Engine

Your airless chutter, your cold consumption,
your push-and-pull, your push-button super-
charge, turbocharger, is not native to
my nose, my mothballed crawler, my purchase
on the underslung world. Mine is inertia,
oil burners, the ring road, gray priming,
scavenging rigid heat. You outdrive me.

We Who Are Happy to Serve You

Trips to New York propose themselves in blue
lines of paper coffee cups,
smelling like trains,
like Diesel fuel and many oils. I wish
you a home by the tracks,
as in Spokane where the freights sighed twice an hour

under our
hotel window, twilight's blue
backdrop or night's black strap, the track
of the moon hitched in the cup
of the coal car's coupling. I wish
you friends better than I, who train

in a town that turned its train
tracks out, its depot now a restaurant, I who never send our
Christmas letters or your birthday cards. I wish
you an Amtrak that leaves at noon's blue,
not at the cat's back of night, as in Salt Lake, the city cupped
by mountains against its inland sea, station a trailer by the light rail
tracks.

I wish you friends with houses near the light rail tracks,
coupling their new condos to the Amtrak trains,
seats that cup
their butts in blue velour. I wish them an hour
with the newspaper, a cup of tea on a blue
plastic tray, your home at the end of the day. I wish

you a beer near the Omaha station. I wish
you a friend in Chicago, its tangle of tracks,
its California Zephyr, its Capitol Limited, its slew of blue
brochures, its Cardinal & Hoosier State, its City of New Orleans,
its opportunity of trains,
its Empire Builder, its Hiawatha, its more-than-every-hour,
its Lake Shore Limited, its Southwest Chief, its Texas Eagle, each
with its own cup

with its own logo at the souvenir stand, own slow slog of regulars
with cups
of Starbucks busying their hands. I wish
you a first-person-plural home, a *we*, an *our*,
as your ex-husband tracks
his eye along the other women, trains
you to distrust *us*. I wish you an end to the blues

of the one-cup dishwasher cycle, ask for you the jazz track
of the wish of distance held in each train's
engine, your arrivals dawning blue.

Rosemary Dunn Moeller
The Lift of Wind Across Wings

The Lift of Wind across Wings

Allowances for balance are
small, brief.
There's so little difference between
too few scoops of coffee grounds and
the perfect amount.
Getting through doorways gracefully,
saying condolences graciously,
twirling plates furiously,
all impossibly determined
by a few grains of time
or grams of speech.

Driving past falling rock zones
I've hoped for that crack,
along the overhanging cantilevered granite,
the thunk of boulder on tree trunk,
a rolling crash after my car passes.
The drama of acrobats and jugglers isn't just
their skill but my desire for destruction,
devastation, tumbling, slicing, burning.

Equilibrium is hubris.

I want to stress out over a small disaster,
attracted by an astral streak across the sky
from some orbit finally disintegrating,
but it's only a meteor.

I've sardonically watched the jawbreakers
rolling around a concave surface at the mall,
waiting to be flushed into the soon-sticky hand of
some temporarily cavity free child.

Balance waits patiently for deconstruction,
waits silently for interruptions
by a symphony of living creatures with all
their beats and croaks and slaps.

Balance slows time to eternity,
focuses sight to a single perspective.
Balance is the breeze across the blue
heron's wings, lifting it in circles.

Rock Picking

Stopping's essential
when I'm in the quarter ton haystack bucket
half a foot above the alfalfa field being planted to corn
picking rocks where a glacier body scrubbed the land
with defoliating granite boulders.

Stopping's executed
by pulling back on the red throttle
back on the eighteen gear shift of the tractor
adjusting the separate hydraulic levers that
lift the bucket, tilt the bucket, raise the claws.

Stopping's immediate
after I signal before jumping off,
not to pick rocks
but beckon him to come down from the cab and look.
Inside a furrow's a neatly woven circle of old grasses
threaded with black downy feathers
holding six duck's eggs in a clutch,
the last one laid, the pearliest.
We mark the spot with a flag—back off, go around, ignore.
Just the right distance from the livestock pond for a clutch of eggs,
just the right number for a black duck to handle.

Earth trembles slightly, pulses erratically all the time,
pushing up broken pieces buried for millennia
for us to gather and move off—earth's eggs
of many colors and densities, scraped from northern shields
dumped where warmer weather curbed the ice rivers' flow,
now thrown in the bucket to go out to the livestock pond
to slow the flow of the creek bed.

Pintail Ducks Doing It in Spring

I'm a voyeur
of mating pintail ducks. This afternoon I only bother
to look east, since the western
view presents a profile, no color
for identifying. But eastward
I watch them come into flooded
fields and swelling creeks. First there's
the grabbing of feathers on the back of her head
by the select one. They whistle or hoarsely quack
before and after like teenagers in an uncomfortable hurry,
ignoring other species who realize what's happening
but don't care. Then
back to feeding, arching his long white neck, dabbling
down for slugs and bugs, like teens popping
cans of almost cold beer, throwing
back their heads, hoping
they hadn't wasted their time.
The angle of the sun orders everything to breed—
fill small nests with eggs by collecting lovers.
Dabbling for strength to mate, to be more than just alive,
to feel more than the temperature change outside,
to feel it inside heads, for a buzzing
or flirting with all their tiny pin feathers,
or the hairs on arms legs bodies
that want to feel
the wet nakedness
somewhere
outside.
I just watch, amazed
that cold dirty water can be a lovers' raft.

I Heard of His Death the Day Whooping Cranes Migrated Past
For Robert Foy, an Extraordinary Teacher and Friend

Nothing occurs at once.
But once upon a time I registered
for a Shakespeare class. You, instructor
working on a dissertation of Biblical Pauline influences
and classical imagery, taught me passionate love
for literature, poetry and myths.
Today "the day's pulled even with the night."
After our forty-four years of advice,
friendship, babysitting kids and gardening for the soul,
I heard you'd died.   But a friend knew where
to go to see whooping cranes migrating,
feeding on waste grains in wetlands along fields.
Of course we went, not to disturb them but to adore.
We parked and waited, resigned to failure,
until they came out. A unique opportunity,
as the almost incomparable
foursome walked, preened, ate and flew off.

Almost incomparable.
One
of your poems provided me the best simile, like
Latona and Zeus, their children Apollo and Diana
captured in stone at Versailles, and by you
Once,
graceful beauty epitomized in water fountain and stone.
And we interrupted the whooping cranes like
Lycians who were turned into frogs,
Their favorite food,
for chasing the gods away from their water.

Four Whooping Cranes,
appropriately crowned, who
might have lingered if Rob had been there to
call them back in Latin, but he's gone now,
and his garden will go to seed and vine, untended.
Whooping cranes may survive, extremely endangered.
They left of their own choosing.

Night Herons on Their Own Expedition

The pair of them perched in a cottonwood
hanging out over the lake, dining and dashing off,
as we do when we're busy.
                              But not today; we're paddling,
canoeing in circles, enjoying the weather as if we'll never leave
or seasons will never change.
                              But not last winter;
we parted from home, migrated south, from Dakota
to Antarctica where black-crowned night heron's perch on rocks.
Our unique voyage, their annual flight down and back;
no wonder the pair are unimpressed by us floating beneath them,
orange jacketed the same as we were in South Georgia,
red-eyes and white breasted just like they were within the
convergence.

We needed so much help and assistance to make the trip,
survive the crossing, explore the icy lands and fog-bound days,
the storms at sea; lifeboats and giant anchors on ships, which
they don't pack or carry. We were guided and herded. They
navigate by genes and streams of air currents carrying clues.

We are pitiful examples of our greatest
achievements in exploration.
They are casual circumnavigators cruising
by our country place, looking down for
delicacies like tasty frogs in this pond.

Envious While Leaving Innis Mor on the Ferry

Gannets follow the ferry back
from the island out of boredom,

shimmering white angels' wings with
a tip of black for mortality.

They don't even bother to feed, just float
and fly, dive and swoop,

confident of their mastery of sea and sky,
until they turn back to the island for low tide,

that social hour,

to strut impressively along crabby shores.
They sleep while floating on the rocking sea,

and maybe while soaring slowly
in concentric circles on thermals,

the envy of this airline traveler, skitter around
where I stumbled on rocks and broken shells.

There are probably no gannets in heaven;
they have no need to go.

Puffins at the Cliffs of Mohr, Ireland
For Helen Holmes, born 1887

My spouse prefers to stay on our prairie farm
but is willing to be dragged by me
to see puffins nesting on the Cliffs of Mohr,
sacred commitment in practice.
I watched them,

thrilled, excited, buoyant by joy which
kept me leaning on barriers, open-mouthed,
with binoculars and camera recording
fuzzy images of clumpy clownish birds,
I feel like a hospital visitor to see a newborn cousin,

a one way celebration of new connections,
new love, new meaning for being here,
here, to see puffins returning to where they hatched.
I compare:
we nest, love heights, sailing, floating.

I am deficient where they excel:
puffins are boats, so buoyant they live at sea
when not breeding and making sounds,
to nest despite storms, razorbills
and "sky fishing" Icelanders who

eat their hearts fresh and raw as delicacies:
the casual cruelty of superior predators.
My emigrant grandmother left this coast,
when famine sent souls to sea

in un-feathered boats, to cross,
hoping for life and continuity,
to find a place as solid
as ancient cliffs comprised of dangerous holds
and fragile nests.

She returns within me now, here,
where beautiful red-footed, yellow stripped,
big billed, stocky puffins stayed on and endured.

Crowded Shores at Dusk on Lake Louise

Sunsets happen across the lake from
where the grill is putting out the smell
of burnt sugar that's mixing into the smell,
from the sand that has perch and bass bones,
broken snail shells, walleye scales,
lost fishing lures on tangled lines attached to
submerged Christmas tree branches almost disintegrated
but still holding some acidic pine oil
that almost covers up the back wind of hay clover
and ponderosa pine needles
where nearby chokecherry leaves hide blackbirds but
not grackles that like the juniper trees that
have the scent of gin above the new mown grass
along the trailhead where a pile of fresh cut
cottonwood logs for
firewood at the campfires is stacked by rangers for
the grills that still have the sticky sweet burnt marshmallow
stuck to the iron bars.

Sunsets are orange and blue experiments
in complementary wheels
of cloud migrations, bird locations
insect destinations, wood chip conflagrations,
all beyond my ability to contain or control,
so I just sit by the fire, watch the end of this sun
and begin a meditation on darkness,
its gifts of illumination.

Sun sets. Moon, already risen
but now clearer although grey shadowed,
waxes, like the tapered candles were waxed repeatedly
that we used in the house when electricity failed,
but not now because there is no failure of power.
The reflective shine of the moon on the water hits my retina
and re-stimulates my memories of fishing by moonlight.
This sound wave throbbing air,
full of molecules of scents and photons of bent
refracted light, leave hardly a place for any more of my sense.

Unused to Dragonflies

Lots of large dragonflies flourish along
our flooded fields,
a disastrous harvest for us,
bountiful breeding grounds for families
of *Odonata* moving in like a rush of
Mediterranean immigrants with multi-syllabic
names all ending in vowels.
Gomphidae fuss around lilac seeds and squash blossoms,
Libellulidae hover within cedars and foxtail grasses
hunting, always hunting, hunting,
then swimming in our creek that never flows in August until
this summer, scattering
eggs that'll freeze in January and hatch in June, long after
mom has rested her wings forever, dad has curled up and died.
But today they're everywhere, in humid ditches
weed green un-disked fields of mud and duck wallows
where we usually have corn growing.
Jewelers, who decorate their images
in multi-colored enamels, flashing stones, are
realists reproducing nature's conspicuous
extravagance.

Mated For Life

Swans are exquisitely beautiful slobs,
with messy nests
reeds and weeds sticking out all over
protruding everywhere
highly visual stimulus packaging
like my littered walls and surfaces at home
souvenirs, pieces of people's connections
passing fancies and treasured tomes of
kitschy novels and second class reference books
jewelry hanging on picture frames,
like moss dragging off their nest.
Goslings don't mind until they grow up
and can't wait to move out of the wet mess
to their own paradise for two
of sticks and shells and breeding among memories.

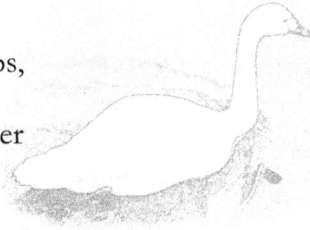

Egret Regrets

Egrets slip down through air, defining grace,
with whiter than martyrs' wings,
and beaks like scholars' knowledgeable looks.
Don't watch them eating bugs or dead fish.

Nature requires no justification for beauty,
needs no similes to survive, abhors explanations.
My awe and amazement, appall,
are worthless in organic currency.

All I can do is be housekeeper. (We live
under the same roof.) Scrub the water,
shake out the air, sweep up the earth.
I do what I can for Sister Egret.

Afternoon Thunderstorm on the Sound

Beachfront renters discuss traffic rotaries,
kids burrow in the sands, throw shells at
brothers, bother adults with demands to take home seaweed.
By four p.m. the Sound's almost empty of people.

Now the black-backed gulls
forage for chips and nuts, protect
their shifting sands from common terns
looking for crumbs, and smaller herring gulls
with nothing better to do than glide

gracefully, land silently and look at the seascape
in surround eye view, as if it could be better
but is acceptable. Waves bring more seaweed to shore,
clung to by shells that will soon be gull gulps,
then child's toys, before sandals crush them to pieces.

Tourists carry the ground up shells
on skin and soles to cars and campers,
until the sand's vacuumed out back home
in a state bordered by states,
unlike this point surrounded

by ocean that'll get back the sand. Flowing,
flowing always toward the waves being washed
as rain comes down, inches of rain falling
into the Sound, fresh and unsalted, warm and hard,
providing loud steady percussion

to the collapsing thunder rolls
chasing after white light bursts
so fierce that the afternoon's illuminated and shaken.
The sandy shore becomes a wet velvet carpet.
The gulls, invisible as wind, have gone back out to sea.

The rumble of rain on the car roof
and thunderous pounding from lightning beating
the sky apart are joyous sounding
as a rock concert audience,
deliriously thrilled by their spectacular show.

Above Pearl Creek

There were no egrets
here when I was born, and I was born
elsewhere.
They found this part of the prairie, this
pasture drained by Pearl Creek,
about fifteen years before I did.
They've made it theirs now,
eating with cattle,
(like farmers in the Chinese restaurant in Huron,
comfortable with the apparently exotic,
familiar pork, beef, chicken),
eating with cattle
that provide them with insect delicacies.

I've changed so much.

I've made it less treeless
trying to keep fruit for sauce.
I've pointed to colored shapes only my urban tinted
lenses could see, drummed
out songs that only my hearing impaired
rhythms of waves on shores could love, discovered
odors only a childhood spent on city buses could
register as unnatural.

The egrets found this prairie and
now it's theirs.
I'm jealous.
I'm looking homeward when
I watch them
lift and float and drift
above my pasture.

Stable Population of Grebes, Least Concern

Stealth paddling the canoe while
five western grebes feed
then all dive I paddle furiously
get closer then freeze in the heat
of July when they surface

They're not fooled. Their calls change
from clacking to long shrill loud directions.
The five dive and spread out, sacrificing security equally
so most will survive. They're not endangered,
but they probably don't know that. I do.
Paddling the canoe
away to give them a break, enjoying
my observations at their distress.

Lake is already full of algae
runoff from pastures where cows graze.
They're not threatened;
they probably don't know that. But I do.
Fertilized fields full of wheat and corn
not a concern. Green is everywhere.
Green algae blooms in the water.
Grebes don't appear to mind the algae,
feeling more threatened by me.

I paddled, husband fished for northern,
caught more than the grebes did.
Northern pike are also ranked least concern. Don't know it.
I do. But the water isn't clear, full of green algae
using up oxygen from the lake.
Slowly suffocating lake life,
slowly running off fertilized grain fields,
slowly flowing downward across our flat prairie.

Black Flight against Blue Sky

Driving's hard on the gravel road
when annoying blackbirds take flight
in aerial acrobatics of form and movement
that defy swarm behaviors of humans
demonstrating superior sensitivity to space.
I veer toward the ditch, correct and give thanks
for the absence of traffic on our back roads.
We need rules, white lines and reflectors
that blackbirds don't use, who hover just
over our cornfields, changing from one to the other
as if we'd invited them, invasive
alien species that we are to this prairie pasture.

This won't last.
It's already freezing cold in the mornings,
frost on the pumpkins I need to take to
the day care center, our nestlings kept occupied
by coloring faces on a perfectly good food supple
that will be smashed in days, like my pickup would
if there were too many of us, thoughtlessly
watching the distracting exaltation of blackbirds

as they flutter and flap, ungraceful compared to geese,
but dancers compared to us while we harvest and drive pickups,
running meals to fields and parts from town.
They curl and curve as if it were fun to be out this fall
when cold breezes and brown leaves are doing their own dance,
when I've forgotten how to balance on the balls of my feet
or to break for wild running pheasants.

Too Many Apples

I need a break from mopping my kitchen floor,
so I'm out on my deck, smelling
rotting apples instead of my own sweat.
They're slowly fermenting with
bugs and worms breaking skin.
Pheasants will feast on them,
first sticking their beaks in, shaking them about
to smash them, then devouring the bug ridden delicacies.
But first I need to shovel
them up. I haven't.
I want the better apples,
ones that still cling to twig and branch,
are still firm and whole,
not these reminders of my procrastinating.
Unfortunately, I need to walk on the rot
that squishes beneath my shoes
to get to them, the higher ups, the ones with a view.
Work was going so well, until I tired of the
apple-peeler-corer marvel machine,
filling bags with two cups of sliced
white goodness, two tbls. of sugar, one c. of flour,
¼ tsp. of cinnamon, and a half stick of butter, oats
and nuts to taste, zip shut and into the freezer
for winter desserts.
I clean the kitchen floor so I can make another mess.
I put up summer's garden so I have home grown food to cook.
Some days the cycle is a celestial epiphany.
Some days it's rotting-apple mush.
Today the pheasants feast.

Perseid's Meteor Shower and Pheasants after Dark

August and the Perseids
mean camp chairs facing
north-east, hoping the moon
won't rise too early
before marvelous streaks
of flaming fiery rocks
flash before us
between periods of quiet anticipation,
broken by the fat flapping sound of pheasants.
Like toddlers that won't quiet down,
they stay out late, making the darkness noisy,
hens fussing,
roosters flying from invaders
to their territory, our cornfields.
Their colors unnoticeable
but their shapes are smoky ghosts
flying just above the tassels.

It's dark and glorious and
we anticipate shooting and ahhing,
shot out stars from
dark skies that absorb
their sounds and ours.
We sit in comfort,
gaze and listen.

Common Grackles in Common (*Quiscalus   quiscula*)

We have grackles in common,
common grackles, in fact, that make their cupped
nests wherever,
(quis quis), whatever.
Are they really yours or ours-- who move
like our "snowbirds" leaving
frozen farms and frosted
fenced fields in February for
visits filled with families
they know from recent
seasons of migrating?
Back here they talk about you,
endlessly cackling, like grackles,
over the strange dress of southerners.
Dakota grackles that winter with you,
love your spring-like Valentine's Days
—not twenty below.
Like grackles, our Dakotans rarely go
to any but small towns.
You think they're your common grackles,
we think they're ours.
They come back to us in summer,
high prairies, higher altitudes and attitudes
of people who are neighborly because
there are so few of our species here.
We have more cedars than seniors.
But in February, we all think
those of us who don't migrate are crazy.

Event Horizon Along the Prairie Road

Leaves in August on honey-locust trees, yellow and orange,
unseasonally strange, drew us out of the field like a burning bush.

Along the prairie road, ruts and bumps cut off
our complete sentences into fragments.

Whole trees dispersed their leaves
in slow motion, horizontally,

flying off which-ways as we gently shut pick-up doors.
Monarchs migrating, information shared mysteriously,

only on the trees' north side, facing the sunflowers,
maybe for food, siesta, or

like travelers meeting hometown relations overseas,
reflecting on the fields orange-black beauty.

We froze so they'd sail
back, settle down, stop time for us.

Yellow wings opened and
folded like external lungs breathing,

magnificence in thousands of maybe-identical butterflies.
We had to start the pick-up. We had

to turn around in the field and
go on up north to another. We had

to miss their
leaving.

Sketching Decaying Leaves

A whitetail deer watches her sitting on a tree stump
sketching the leaves under her feet that
move in the slight wind that
gently musses her hair.

She has plans to go to medical school
after she goes to the U
after she graduates high school
after she gets her driver's license
after she brings up her grades
so doing well in art class means
a lot to her.

She's not sure why, but she likes drawing dead things,
aspen leaves and owl pellets at her feet.
There was a dead possum by the roadside.
After the rest of the class walked around it
in revulsion, she stopped, got her cell phone
and took nine photos,
poking it with her foot to get the other side,
mouth open, teeth bared,
tongue hanging into the dirt,
fur matted with blood.

She decided to draw a
dead sparrow instead,
half buried in the decayed aspen leaves at her feet,
half eaten by something else
also interested in dead things.

Drought Defiance in Blue, While on the Road in Mali

The paved road to Baguineda,
to Baguineda, passes by schools and shops,
shops that are new,
new homes with solid walls, tin roofs,
tin roofs above running water in pipes and
dependable electricity,
electrical miracle of twenty-first century
engineering, throughout an ancient landscape,
landscape of bizarrely shaped red stone boulders,
boulders along fields of edibles, irrigated,
irrigated green and fertile and growing,
a multitude of loaves from bushels of seeds,
and banquets of fish from the Niger,
the Niger River, flowing
anew, creating stomach-filling
livelihoods for farmers and villagers. And
amid the dried leaves and downed grain
are beautiful red-checked bluebirds,
picking and feeding as they have for ages,
for ages weaving grassy domed nests on trees,
for ages, on flamboyant trees that are a blaze of
glorious red spatters across
blue skies above the green and fertile
growing fields, on the old earth,
the earth that's struggled and starved for decades,
and now breathes moister air from softer farm ground.
Their cordon-bleu color stands apart
from the sky, from water holes and
blue painted houses, unique.
Their cordon-bleu songs are part of the heart
beating heated air of the Sahel. *Tsee-tsee.*
Today, all is well.

Attracted by Futile Tapping in Winter

Magnetic tapping helps me locate
the woodpecker's tree,
to listen to futile winter drilling
for useless dead food. But instinct, like drumming
with a spoon on the kitchen counter
to relieve stress,
relieves the need to make noise.
I'm here, alone, anxious, waiting for
recovery, normalcy.
Instinct likes normalcy,
a Zen level of activity
even if it's drumming a regular
beat on a dead cottonwood tree trunk or
with a dead wooden spoon by the kitchen window.
The woodpecker won't eat much.
I'm useless as the dead bugs in the tree
are for her nourishment,
helpless, as the drumming of my fingers are
on the visitor's chair in his hospital room.
Not waiting or visiting,
just following instincts.

Stirring the Pot

Blue jays abound this autumn
in barren bushes along ditches,
tree strips and lone orchards.
Unfairly attractive for such

distasteful personalities—
thieves, bullies, off-key screamers.
Fields full of ripe sorghum are
insufficient.

Gender equality in color and intelligence
manifests in cooperative attacks,
planning caches,
maneuvering for all space on feeders.

Unlike the blackbird cousins,
theirs is a beautiful aggression,
entrances are militaristic
with fake alarms

and unnecessary bravado.
Unfairly beautiful, unfairly intelligent
unfair for the less courageous.
Aggression seems personal, no higher

motivation than satisfaction.
Like the wooden spoon that stirs the stew, unfair
to carrots trying to settle on the bottom
and burn.

Addicted to Ashes

(Habit is habit, and not to be flung out the window
by any man but coaxed down stairs a step at a time.
—Mark Twain)

Grackles fall down our chimney
get caught, flapping, crying
just like our lab, Shadow, cries
to get at them in the cooled fireplace
to play with them, bite them
ashes and all.
We've devised a system of open doors
to the outside,
barricaded doors
to inner rooms
sounds we make as we flail our arms
to get the birds outside
while our dog jumps and barks
thrilled by the game.
Sometimes the grackle wins escape
sometimes Shadow gets her mouth full of feathers
always I wish they wouldn't fall down.
Outside, in the junipers, grackles shimmer in the light
and caw angrily at everything mammalian.
They look just as natural
covered in ashes and flailing hopelessly
above open doors, like bad habits that need
to be coaxed outside.
But they keep coming back down
to be dealt with again and again,
their purple iridescent throats
like polished stones in my necklaces,
their annoying stumbles
a threatening addiction.

To Here from the Plains of *Shinar*

I can't just gaze in admiration of red-orange berries
in September but must identify "mountain ash tree."
I don't just listen and watch a feathered colony
eating those orange-red berries but think "robins."
I name them for the illusion that I possess the scene.

But if I say I saw *shishokah* dancing up and down
in the *pseti can* I possess nothing.
Lakota isn't my language although spoken here
long before I opened my eyes.

I don't easily forget the Latin for *Turdus migratorius,*
unfairly named little orange-beaked brown-backed beauty.

Latin doesn't seem foreign although
millennia and leagues away from where I feel at home.

Sorbus americanus reminds me of delicious orange
sorbet, mnemonics for memory of mountain ash.

I have crossed oceans and
continents to find this place at this time.

I name to remember, name to pause and inhale
this moment into my body, to in-corporate

what feathers and berries I can before this season
and scene cease, when I will be left behind

with less color, less music, with only
dry branches and feathers on the ground.

The Plains of Shinar: where the mythical Tower of Babel was built
Shishokah (Lakota); Turdus migratorius (Latin): robin
Pseti can (Lakota);Sorbus americanus(Latin): mountain ash